Message Received!

Sharon Coan

D1402863

Consultants

Sally Creel, Ed.D.
Curriculum Consultant

Leann Iacuone, M.A.T., NBCT, ATC
Riverside Unified School District

Jill Tobin
California Teacher of the Year
Semi-Finalist
Burbank Unified School District

Image Credits: p.12 (inset) Australia/Bigstock p.5
Beverley Vycital/Getty Images; p.24 Cultura/Igore/
Getty Images; pp.4, 7, 12 (bottom)–13 chris2766/
iStock; pp.20–21 (illustrations) Janelle Bell-Martin;
all other images from Shutterstock.

Library of Congress Cataloging-in-Publication Data

Coan, Sharon, author.
  Message received! / Sharon Coan, M.S.Ed.; consultants
Sally Creel, Ed.D. curriculum consultant, Leann Iacuone,
M.A.T., NBCT, ATC, Riverside Unified School District,
Jill Tobin, California Teacher of the Year Semi-Finalist,
Burbank Unified School District.
      pages cm
  Summary: "Sight and sound help us understand the
world around us. Sounds travel to our ears. We see images
with our eyes. How else do your ears and eyes work
together?"— Provided by publisher.
  Audience: K to grade 3.
  Includes index.
  ISBN 978-1-4807-4565-0 (pbk.)
  ISBN 978-1-4807-5055-5 (ebook)
  1. Senses and sensation—Juvenile literature.
  2. Hearing—Juvenile literature.
  3. Vision—Juvenile literature.
  4. Perception—Juvenile literature. I. Title.
  QP434.C55 2015
  152.1—dc23
                                        2014013150

Teacher Created Materials
5301 Oceanus Drive
Huntington Beach, CA 92649-1030
http://www.tcmpub.com
ISBN 978-1-4807-4565-0
© 2015 Teacher Created Materials, Inc.
Made in China
Nordica.082015.CA21501181

Table of Contents

At the Animal Shelter 4

The Ears Hear It! 10

The Eyes See It! 14

Time to Choose. 18

Let's Do Science! 20

Glossary. 22

Index 23

Your Turn!. 24

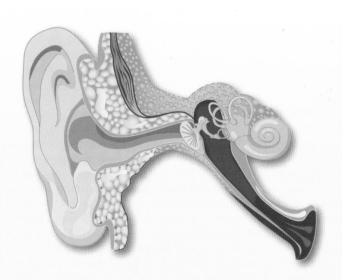

At the Animal Shelter

It is noisy! There is so much to see! You do not know where to look first. You are at the animal shelter to get a new pet. Which one will you choose?

Animal shelters have many types of pets.

5

You hold a soft kitten. She purrs quietly in your arms. You hear a puppy, "Yip, yip, yip!" His tail is wagging quickly. A colorful parrot catches your eye. It squawks, "Hello! Hello!"

Your ears and eyes are really busy. So is your brain. Your ears and eyes collect many sounds and sights. Your brain figures out what they are.

You hear a hamster wheel spinning.

You hear dogs barking.

You see a cat.

The Ears Hear It!

A lot of your ear is inside your head. The part of the ear on the outside is shaped like a **funnel**.

funnel

Only a small part of your ear can be seen.

The funnel collects sound waves. It directs them down the ear canal. At the end, the sound waves bump the **eardrum**. The eardrum starts to **vibrate** (VAHY-breyt).

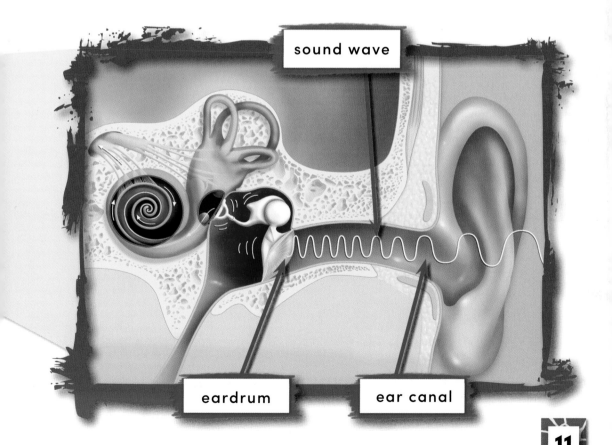

sound wave

eardrum

ear canal

The **vibrations** (vahy-BREY-shuhnz) make the tiny bones inside your ear move. The bones pass the vibrations to the inner ear.

purrrr

eardrum

ear canal

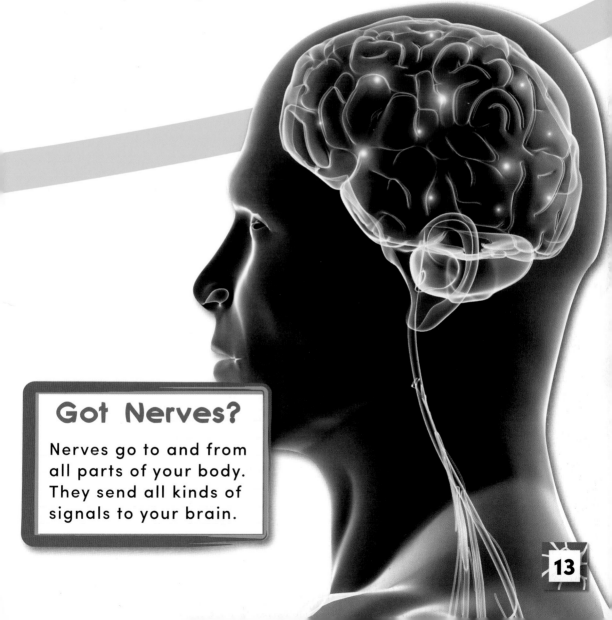

There, the vibrations are turned into **nerve** signals (SIG-nlz) that go to your brain. Your brain makes sense of those signals. You think, "I hear a kitten purring."

Got Nerves?

Nerves go to and from all parts of your body. They send all kinds of signals to your brain.

The Eyes See It!

Like the ear, most of your eye is inside your head.

pupil

Light passes into the back of your eye through the **pupil**.

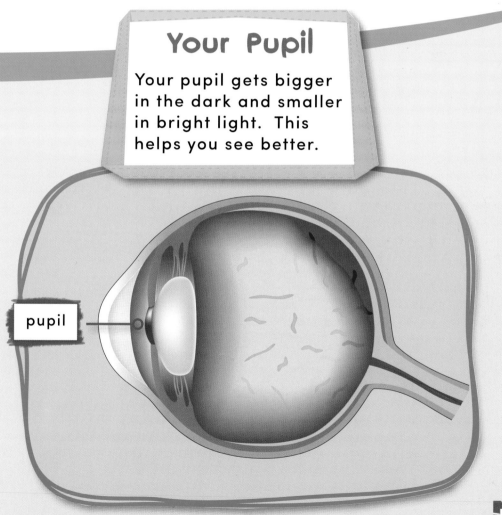

Your Pupil

Your pupil gets bigger in the dark and smaller in bright light. This helps you see better.

pupil

Inside your eye, light is turned into nerve signals. The signals flow to the brain. The **image** (IM-ij) arrives in your brain upside down! But, do not worry, your smart brain turns the image right side up and tells you what it is. You see a colorful parrot!

The parrot looks upside down to your brain. Then, your brain flips the image.

Time to Choose

Whew! What a lot of work your ears and eyes and brain have done. These senses will help you choose your pet. What will it be?

Let's Do Science!

How do sight and sound work together? Try this and see!

What to Get

- ○ 4 clear water glasses
- ○ food coloring
- ○ spoon
- ○ water

What to Do

1 Fill each glass with a different amount of water. Add a different color of food coloring to each glass.

1

2 Strike each glass gently with the spoon. What do you see? What do you hear?

2

3 Strike the glasses to make a tune. Use the colors to tell a friend how to play the tune.

3

Glossary

eardrum—a little piece of skin in the ear that sound waves hit

funnel—a cone-shaped object that directs things from the large end to the small end

image—a picture

nerve—a bundle of fibers that carries messages between parts of the body and the brain

pupil—the small, black, round area at the center of the eye

vibrate—to move back and forth very fast

vibrations—fast back and forth movements

Index

brain, 8, 13, 16–18

ears, 8, 10–14, 18, 24

eye, 6, 8, 14–16, 18, 24

kitten, 6, 13

nerve, 13, 16

parrot, 6, 16–17

puppy, 6

Your Turn!

Sights and Sounds

Think about how your ears and eyes work together. Keep a journal. Make notes about where you hear interesting sounds. Draw pictures of the things you see that make the sounds.